Table of Contents

Waimea Canyon, Kaua`i

Introduction

The Hawaiian archipelago, stretching 1600 miles across the North Pacific Ocean, is one of the most isolated areas on Earth. Located more than 2500 miles form the nearest continent, this spectacular group of islands has the world's highest percentage of unique terrestrial species. Nearly 97% of Hawaii's native organisms are found nowhere else on the globe. Their are nearly 1000 species of native plants, approximately 135 different types of native birds and at least 5000 insect forms found in the Aloha State. This miracle of evolution was made possible by the combined forces of time, extreme isolation, diversified terrain, and the adaptive capabilities of newly arrived continental species.

Occupying just 0.2% of the total land of the United States, Hawai`i has several more, albeit unfortunate, environmental distinctions. The state is the extinction capital of the nation and accounts for over 72% of our countries extirpated species. The islands are in the midst of an ecological catastrophe while the world is losing one of its most beautiful, evolutionary masterpieces.

Many factors have contributed to this great environmental destruction. These include habitat loss due to agricultural, residential and commercial development; predation of native species by introduced cats, rats, and mongoose; severe forest damage by non-native pigs, goats, cattle, sheep and deer; competition from introduced plants and birds; and avian diseases such as malaria and pox. Perhaps the most regrettable factor contributing to this natural holocaust is widespread public apathy and lack of care for the environment.

My intention for this book is to provide the reader with images of Hawaii's diverse and colorful endemic species that hopefully will inspire some to explore the island's remaining native forests. I have selected only a very small number of species to portray from amongst a biota of immeasurable diversity. Perhaps anyone who might observe and experience these unique organisms will be moved by their sublime magnificence and be motivated to help defend their right to exist. The environmental community needs everyone's concern, participation, and support to prevent any more of this grave loss. It is both our responsibility and moral duty to preserve the native Hawaiian species that remain for all future generations to behold.

Dedication

This book is dedicated to my brother Mark, who is both a great friend and brother in every sense of the word. His generosity, kindness and wisdom has enriched my life and made this book possible.

Hanalei Bay, Kaua`i

Photo by Mark Walther, 1980

Preface

This book is separated into sections covering native plants and birds with several representative species from the dry forest, subalpine scrubland and montane wet forest natural communities. Most of the organisms portrayed are common and can be easily found by any serious observer. The majority of photographs are of species which can be seen in the wet forests of Kaua`i and Maui, places where I have most often visited. Space limitations prevent a more comprehensive coverage of habitats and species. Each portrait is accompanied with a Hawaiian name, if one exists, scientific name, description, and occurrence information. I have included a section on some of the threats to our native flora and fauna as well as a list of nonprofit environmental organizations and government wildlife agencies. Please support those who are working to preserve Hawaii's environment.

Mahalo,

Michael Walther

Michael Walther
Honolulu, Hawaii
January 1, 1996

As recently as 1968 all six of these unique Hawaiian native forest birds survived on Kaua`i. From left to right, Kaua`i `O`o (*Moho braccatus*), Kaua`i `Akialoa (*Hemignathus procerus*), `O`u (*Psittirostra psittacea*), Kaua`i Nukupu`u (*Hemignathus l. hanapepe*), Puaiohi (*Myadestes palmeri*), and Kamao (*Myadestes myadestinus*). Today the `O`o, `Akialoa, `O`u and Kamao are either extinct or very close to extinction while the Puaiohi and Nukupu`u are extremely rare. Sadly, the only place a person can now see most of these species are in the dark, ominous cabinets of the Bishop Museum Collection room.

Cyanea sylvestris, Kaua'i

KOKI`O `ULA `ULA

Hibiscus kokio

subsp. *saintjohnianus*

This beautiful native Hawaiian hibiscus is found as either a shrub or small tree from 9 to 21 feet tall. The flowers are a bright orange red or rarely, yellow. This species is found in both dry and wet forests on O`ahu, Maui, Moloka`i and Kaua`i from 200 - 3000 feet. The subspecies above, saintjohnianus, can best be seen on the Nualolo Cliff trail in July and August when it's spectacular flowers bloom. This subspecies is considered rare.

MA `O HAUHELE

Hibiscus brackenridgei

subsp. *mokuleianus*

Hibiscus brackenridgei, is Hawaii's state flower. Growing as shrubs 3 -9 feet tall this native plant has distinctive yellow flowers with purple spots at the inside base of the petals. Considered rare the Ma`o hauhele grows in the shrublands and dry forests on all the main islands except Kaho`olawe and Ni`ihau. One of the best locations to observe this species is in the Waiane mountains of O`ahu.

KOKI`O KE`OKE`O

Hibiscus waimeae
subsp. *waimeae*

A third type of native hawaiian hibiscus is the beautiful white *H. waimeae* which grows on the steep, dry cliffs of Waimea Canyon, Kaua`i. The trees, which attain a height of 18 to 30 feet, can be seen on the canyon trail below Waipoo Falls. The flowers bloom during the summer and fall and have a light fragrance. This species occurs from 750 - 3,600 feet in the valleys of northwest Kaua`i. Another native white hibiscus, *H. arnottianus*, grows in the Ko`olau Mountains of O`ahu.

WILIWILI

Erythrina sandwicensis

One of the most beautiful native trees of the dry forest, this species grows as high as 45 feet. It is considered locally abundant and can be found up to 1500 feet elevation on the leeward sides of all the main islands. The flowers are orange, yellow or green. This tree can also be identified by it's distinctive reddish bark. Early Hawaiians used the light wood of the Wiliwili for surf-boards and fishing floats. One of the best places to view this native tree is along Koke`e road between Kekaha and Koke`e State Park, Kaua`i. The colorful blossoms are abundant in June, July, and August.

MOA

Psilotum nudum

Moa is a fairly common component of dry shrublands and occurs on all the main islands. A great place to observe this species is the Nature Conservancy's Kapunakea Preserve on West Maui. Attaining a height of one foot, *Psilotum nudum* can grow either on the ground, amongst rocks, or as an epiphyte on tree branches. Early Hawaiians used this primitive plant to make tea.

`AHINAHINA

Artemisia australis

This species is a strongly aromatic plant that also occurs in the dry low elevation shurblands on Maui. Ahinahina can be found on all the main islands. *Artemisia australis* usually grows on cliffs. An excellent place to see this native plant are the foothills of West Maui.

`OHI`A LEHUA

Metrosideros polymorpha

This is the most common tree in Hawaii's native forests. The `Ohi`a can be found in many shapes and sizes as its scientific name suggests, attaining heights from 100 foot giants to one foot dwarfs that grow on montane, wet bogs. The most noticeable characteristic of this tree is its brilliant, scarlet flowers. Found on all the main islands except Ni`ihau and Kaho`olawe, this species provides abundant nectar to many types of native Hawaiian honeycreepers. A great place to view spectacular `Ohi`a trees is at Hakalau National Wildlife Refuge on Hawai`i.

KOA

Acacia koa

The second most common tree occurring in the Hawaiian native forest is this majestic species which can attain heights of over 115 feet. The leaves are sickle shaped and the flowers cream colored. Koa wood attains a beautiful luster when cut and polished and is used in the manufacture of valuable bowls and furniture. Early Hawaiians used large trunks of Koa to make ocean going canoes. Because of ranching and the sugar industry, this species has been reduced significantly. Trees can still be found from 200 to 6000 feet on all the main islands except Ni`ihau and Kaho`olawe. Several excellent places for viewing groves of Koa are Koke`e State Park, Kaua`i, Tantalus trail, O`ahu and Hakalau National Wildlife Refuge on the Island of Hawai`i.

`OLAPA

Cheirodendron trigynum

This is another native tree of the Hawaiian forest and can be identified by its bright green leaves that always seem to be moving, even in a very light wind. The `Olapa grows from 15-45 feet tall and occurs in both mesic and wet areas on all the major islands except Kaho`olawe. The berries of this tree are eaten by several species of native Hawaiian birds including the rare Puaiohi. The bark, leaves and fruit were used by Hawaiians to make a blue dye. An excellent place to see the `Olapa is on the Pihea trail,  Alaka`i Wilderness Preserve, Kaua`i.

LOULU

Pritchardia minor

There are 19 species of this native Palm found in Hawai`i, 11 of which are either rare or endangered. The specimen above was photographed in the Alaka`i Wilderness Preserve on Kaua`i from the Pihea trail. The Loulu occurs on Hawai`i, Maui, Kaua`i, Ni`ihau, Moloka`i, and Oahu in very limited numbers. Introduced rats which eat the fruit of these trees, are causing reproductive failure in many species.

MAMANE

Sophora chrysophylla

Sophora chrysophylla is a common component of the subalpine scrubland natural community and can be found on all the main islands except Kaho`olawe and Ni`ihau. It grows as a shrub or tree to over 45 feet tall with bright yellow flowers which allow for easy identification. Several places to observe this species are Haleakala National Park on Maui and the slopes of Mauna Loa Volcano, Hawaii. When the Mamane is in bloom Hawaiian forest birds can be found feeding on the abundant nectar.

AKALA

Rubus hawaiiensis

This beautiful native plant, also known as the Hawaiian Raspberry, produces a bright red fruit that is edible but somewhat bitter. The Akala grows as shrubs which attain heights of 4 -10 feet. This species can be found on Kauai, Maui, Molokai and Hawai`i. Early Hawaiians obtained a dye from the berries and flowers of *Rubus hawaiiensis*. The Akala has very small thorns and is highly susceptible to grazing pressure of feral ungulates.

PUKIAWE

Styphelia tameiameiae

Styphelia tameiameiae is a very common plant which occurs on all the main islands except Ni`ihau and Kaho`olawe growing from 900 to 7000 feet. Pukiawe is highly adaptable and can be found in dry, wet or boggy habitats. One of the best places to see this species is in the subalpine shrublands of Haleakala National Park.

`OHELO

Vaccinium calycinum

`Ohelo grows as a small shrub 3 -15 feet tall. The most conspicuous characteristic used to identify this native plant are the bright red, edible berries that are between 1/2 and 3/4 inch in diameter. Occurring from 1500 to 6000 feet, this species can be found on all the main islands except Ni`ihau and Kaho`olawe. Hawaiians consider the related species, *Vaccinium reticulatum*, sacred to the goddess Pele. A great place to see `Ohelo is at Hawai`i Volcanoes National Park on the Island of Hawai`i.

PILO

Coprosma montana

Mountain pilo grows as either a small tree or shrub and can attain a height of 6 - 24 feet. The most noticeable characteristic of this species are the small, bright orange berries. Coprosma montana is a common element of the subalpine shrubland vegetation community, and can be found growing on East Maui and the Big Island of Hawai`i.

KOLI`I

Trematolobelia kauaiensis

The Koli`i is one of the most beautiful native plants in Hawai`i. When it blooms in the late summer this species is covered with bright, scarlet flowers which act like magnets to hawaiian forest birds drawn to the abundant nectar. Growing only on Kaua`i, *Trematolobelia kauaiensis* can be observed from the Pihea trail in the Alaka`i Wilderness Preserve. Another species, *T. macrostachys,* occurs on O`ahu, Moloka`i, Maui and in the Kohala Mountains of Hawai`i.

Hāhā

Cyanea sylvestris

One of several spectacular cyaneas growing only on Kaua`i is *Cyanea sylvestris*. The tubular shaped flowers are white with a purplish stripe. The Amakihi, a native hawaiian honeycreeper, often obtains nectar from this plant. One of the best locations to see this beautiful species is along upper Kawaikoi stream above the Alaka`i trail crossing on Kaua`i.

Hāhā LUA

Cyanea leptostegia

The Haha lua is one of the most easily observed Cyaneas and can be found growing next to the canyon trail on Kaua`i. This species, which looks like a palm, grows from 9 to over 40 feet tall.

Hāhā

Cyanea hirtella

Another species of the lobelia family occurring only on Kaua`i is *Cyanea hirtella*. This shrub grows to between 3 -18 feet and is found in the high, wet forest of the Garden Island. There are 62 types of cyaneas found in Hawai`i. The *Campanulaceae* family, of which the cyaneas are part, represent one of the best examples of adaptive radiation in Hawaiian native plants. Unfortunately, nearly 30% of the species belonging to this group are now extinct.

LIMU

Rizogonium punges

This is a very common moss species that grows in the wet forests of all the islands except for Ni`ihau and Kaho`olawe. Found on the ground, rocks and on trees, Limu is a name Hawaiians gave to all types of mosses, lichens and algae. When sunlight filters thru the forest canopy to illuminate *Rhizogonium pungens*, it shines with great beauty.

`AMA`U

Sadleria cyatheoides

The `Ama`u is a very common tree fern that occurs on all the main islands. It grows to over five feet tall and has red fronds when young that turn green as the plant matures. Some of the best areas to observe this native fern are Haleakala National Park, Maui and Hawai`i Volcanoes National Park on the Big Island of Hawai`i.

`OHE NAUPAKA

Scaevola glabra

This species grows as a small shrub between 4 and 12 feet tall and produces beautiful, bright yellow flowers. `Ohe naupaka occurs in the very wet forests on both Kaua`i and O`ahu. An excellent place to see this native plant is on the Alaka`i swamp trail, Kaua`i.

`IE`IE

Freycinetia arborea

The `Ie`ie is a common woody climber of the native Hawaiian rainforest. The easiest identifying characteristic of this species is the salmon-orange, oblong spikes which are pollinated by both native and alien birds. This plant can be found on all the main Hawaiian islands, except Ni`ihau and Kaho`olawe, from 900 - 4500 feet. The roots of the `Ie`ie were used to make intricately woven baskets by early Hawaiians. An excellent location to view `Ie`ie is the summit of the Ko`olau mountains, O`ahu which can be reached by following the Poamoho and several other trails.

Native Hawaiian Forest Birds

KAUA`I `ELEPAIO

Chasiempis s. sclateri

Of all the native birds in the islands, the `Elepaio is the species a visitor to the forest can most easily see. Especially on Kaua`i these birds will often approach a hiker to within several feet. Hawaii's only flycatcher eats mainly insects and can be found in the forest understory and sometimes on the ground. This species is considered by Hawaiians to be the spiritual guardian of canoe builders. The `Elepaio is doing well on both Kaua`i and Hawai`i but is in serious decline on O`ahu. One of the best areas to observe this curious and friendly native bird is Koke`e State Park on the garden isle of Kaua`i.

`I`IWI

Vestiaria coccinea

The bright crimson `I`iwi is one of the most beautiful Hawaiian forest birds. It is also a great example of the co-evolution that developed between the Aloha State's native honeycreepers and lobeliods. The light colored bill is used to feed on the tubular shaped flowers of the native lobelias and other members of the *Campanulaceae* family. This species is fairly common on Kaua`i, Hawai`i and East Maui but is considered very rare and possibly extinct on West Maui, Oahu, and Molokai. It no longer occurs on Lanai where it was formerly common. The `I`iwi is very vocal and its call has been compared to a rusty, squeaking gate. Early Hawaiians made extensive use of the bird's bright red feathers in the making of their royal cloaks and capes. When captain Cook landed on Kaua`i in 1778 the natives brought him several `I`iwis impaled on a sharp stick as a gift.

KAUA`I `AMAKIHI

Hemingnathus virens stejnegeri

This is another common native forest bird which can be recognized by its yellow-green plumage and long, sharply pointed beak. The `Amakihi is found on Hawai`i, Kaua`i, Maui, Moloka`i and O`ahu, but it is believed to be extinct on Lana`i. This species' diet, which consists of insects, fruit, and nectar can be often seen feeding on flowers of several introduced plants including lantana, blackberry and banana poka. Great places to see the `Amakihi are the Pihea, Awaawapuhi, Nualolo and Alaka`i swamp trails on Kaua`i.

`APAPANE

Himatione s. sanguinea

This bright red honeycreeper is the most common native Hawaiian forest bird and can be found on all the major islands. The plumage is scarlet and black and when the `Apapane flies a patch of white can be seen. It is best distinguished from the `I`iwi, by its black bill. This species is omnivorous, feeding on insects and nectar. The trails of Koke`e State Park, Kaua`i and Hosmer's grove, Maui are excellent locations to see this beautiful species.

`ALAUAHIO

Paroreomyza m. newtoni

This species is also called the Maui creeper and is only found in the high elevation forests of East Maui. Less then 100 years ago it was also common on West Maui and Lana`i but is now extinct in these two locations. The `Alauahio forages on insects while travelling through the canopy in small flocks. These birds can be easily observed at Hosmer's Grove, Haleakala National Park, Maui.

`ANIANIAU

Hemignathus parvus

This beautiful yellow native forest bird is only found on Kaua`i. It is a fairly common species that can be easily seen on the trails of Koke`e State Park and in the Alaka`i Wilderness Preserve. As seen in this photograph the `Anianiau feeds on nectar but also forages for insects.

PUAIOHI

Myadestes palmeri

The secretive and mysterious Puaiohi is one of the rarest native Hawaiian forest birds. Scientists believe that less then fifty individuals of this species survive in the high, wet forests of Kaua`i. Found nowhere else on earth the small Kaua`i thrush, as it is also called, has been in decline for over 100 years. When discovered in 1892, the Puaiohi was considered very common and occurred everywhere on the Garden Island. During the last century the population has been severely reduced because of avian malaria, predation by cats and rats, competition with alien birds, hunting, collecting and destruction of habitat.

Threats to the
Native Forest Species

DEVELOPMENT ON NATIVE FORESTS

Many of Hawaii's original native forests have been destroyed, especially in the coastal and low elevation areas to make room for housing, industrial and agricultural developments. This can be seen best on O`ahu where tremendous growth has destroyed almost all of the original lowland dry forest.

40

OVERGRAZING

Overgrazing by feral goats, sheep, deer and cattle result in forest destruction and severe erosion. Much of Hawaii's original native vegetation was lost due to the uncontrolled foraging of hundreds of thousands of introduced grazing animals.

41

NON-NATIVE TREES

In an effort to halt this erosion and to protect valuable watersheds, foresters planted thousands of introduced trees. These included vast plantations of Eucalyptus, silk oaks, and redwood. Most of the native Hawaiian forest bird species have not adapted to the alien forests.

INVASIVE ALIEN SPECIES

Many alien plants have invaded Hawaii's once pristine native forests and are destroying the original inhabitants. The Banana poka (*Passiflora mollissima*) is a very dangerous pest plant that eventually smothers its host tree by cutting off its supply of light.

43

INVASIVE ALIEN SPECIES

Kahili ginger (*Hedychium gardnerianum*), a native of the Himalayas, was introduced into the Hawaiian forest and is now overtaking large areas in the Koke`e area of Kaua`i. The plants, which grow very close together, clog streams and disrupt their ecological function.

INVASIVE ALIEN SPECIES

Many other alien species are causing severe damage to the native forest. These include, left, Glorybush (Tibouchina urvilleana) introduced from Brazil in 1910 and, right foreground, Black Wattle (*Acacia mearnsii*), introduced from Australia in 1890.

INVASIVE ALIEN SPECIES

Two more very serious pest plants are, top, Lantana (*Lantana camara*) introduced from tropical America in 1858 and, bottom, Blackberry (*Rubus argutus*) introduced from Florida.

PREDATION

Hawaii's native plants and birds are also being assaulted by predatory rats that infest the forests. In some places, biologists are trying to eliminate these serious pests by using poison bait stations. Three species of rats have been introduced to Hawaii, the Polynesian rat (*Rattus exulans*), Black rat (*Rattus rattus*) and the Norway rat (*Rattus norvegicus*). Feral cats (*Felis catus*) and mongoose (*Herpestes auropunctatus*) are also serious predators of Hawaii's native birds.

47

INTRODUCED INSECTS

The native insect fauna has been seriously altered by the introduction, both accidental and intentional, of alien insects into the Hawaiian ecosystem. The honey bee hive pictured here is located in the Alaka`i wilderness Preserve, Kaua`i. Like the mosquito, honey bees were introduced to Hawai`i.

NON-NATIVE FOREST BIRDS

Many species of alien birds, such as the very common Japanese white eye (*Zosterops japonicus*) pictured above, have been released into Hawaii's forests. Alien birds compete for food and space with the native species and are believed to be a major factor in their decline.

NON-NATIVE FOREST BIRDS

Newly introduced birds, like this Northern cardinal (*Cardinalis cardinalis*) brought serious diseases, including Avian Malaria and pox, for which the endemic forest birds have no immunity. Scientists believe these lethal maladies are the most important factor contributing to the severe decline of Hawai`i's unique native avifauna.

Napali Coast, Kaua`i

Hawaiian Environmental Organizations

Conservation Council for Hawai`i
P.O. Box 2923, Honolulu, HI 96802 (808) 236•2234

Earthtrust
737 Bishop St. #170-51, Honolulu, HI 96734 (808) 254•2866

Hawai`i Audubon Society
1088 Bishop St. Suite 808, Honolulu, HI 96813 (808) 528•1432

Hawai`i Ho`olau Hou - Hawai`i Releaf
P.O. Box 1209 Lawai, Kaua`i 96765

Hawai`i Nature Center
2131 Makiki Heights Drive, Honolulu, HI 96822 (808) 955•0100

Koke`e Natural History Museum
P.O. Box 100, Kekaha, HI 96752 (808) 335•9975

Life of the Land
1111 Bishop St., Suite 511, Honolulu, HI (808) 533•3454

Native Hawaiian Plant Society
P.O. Box 5021, Kahului, HI 96732

National Tropical Botanical Garden
P.O. Box 340, Lawai, Kaua`i, HI 96765 (808) 332•7324

The Nature Conservancy of Hawai`i
1116 Smith Street, Suite 201, Honolulu, HI 96817 (808) 537•4508

Sierra Club Legal Defense Club
223 S, King St. Suite 400, Honolulu, HI 96813 (808) 599•2436

Sierra Club, Hawai`i Chapter
P.O. Box 2577, Honolulu, HI 96803 (808) 538•6616

U.S. Fish and Wildlife Service
300 Ala Moana Blvd., Honolulu, HI 96850
(808) 541•1201

National Biological Service
P.O. Box 44, Hawaii Volcanos National Park, HI 96718
(808) 967•7396

National Park Service
300 Ala Moana Blvd., Room 6305, Honolulu, HI 96850
(808) 541•2693

Hawaii Department of Land and Natural Resources
1151 Punchbowl Street, Honolulu, HI 96813
(808) 587•0320

University of Hawaii
Department of Zoology
Honolulu, Hawaii
(808) 956•8617

University of Hawaii
Dept. of Botany
(808)956•8369

Bishop Museum
1525 Bernice Street
P.O. Box 19000
Honolulu, HI 96817-0916
(808) 847•3511

Hawaii's Remaining Native Forests

On the following island maps, native forest areas are depicted in black lettering corresponding to each forest or preserve depicted in green. Visitors should contact the Hawai`i Department of Land and Natural Resources, Division of Forestry and Wildlife, U.S. National Park Service, U.S. Fish and Wildlife Service or the Nature Conservancy of Hawai`i for access and tour information.

Island of Hawaii
A- Kohala Mountains
B- Hamakua/Hakalau National Wildlife refuge
C- Puna Area
D- Hawai`i Volcanoes National Park
E- South Kona Mountains
F- Hualalai Volcano

Island of Maui
G- West Maui Mountains/Kapunakea Nature Conservancy Preserve
H- Haleakala National Park/ Waikamoi Nature Conservancy Preserve/
   Hosmer's Grove

Island of Kauai
I- Anahola Mountain
J- Makaleha Mountains
K- Ha`upu Range
L- Alaka`i Wilderness Preserve/ Koke`e State Park
M- Namolokama Mountain

Island of Oah`u
N- Ko`olau Mountains
O- Waianae Mountains/Honouliuli Nature Conservancy Preserve

Island of Moloka`i
P- Nature Conservancy Olokui Preserve
Q- Nature Conservancy Kamakou Preserve

Island of Lana`i
R- Lanaihale

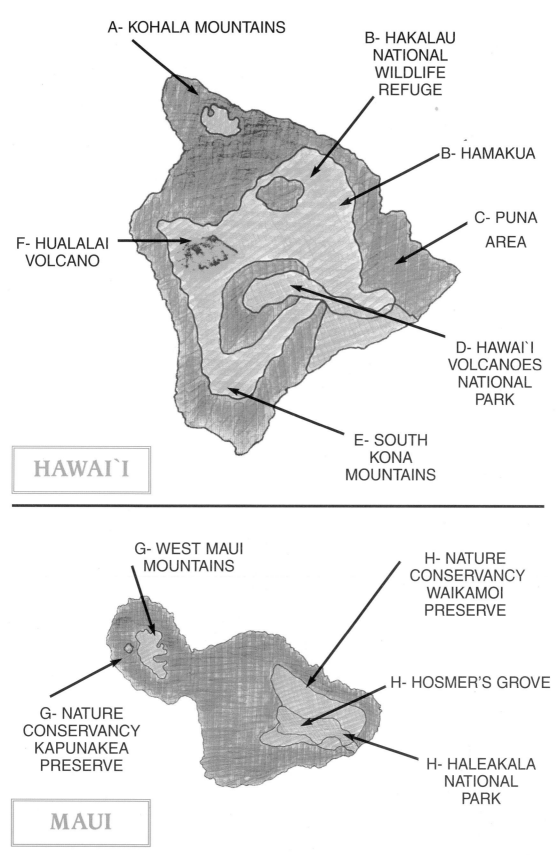

A- KOHALA MOUNTAINS

B- HAKALAU NATIONAL WILDLIFE REFUGE

B- HAMAKUA

C- PUNA AREA

F- HUALALAI VOLCANO

D- HAWAI`I VOLCANOES NATIONAL PARK

E- SOUTH KONA MOUNTAINS

HAWAI`I

G- WEST MAUI MOUNTAINS

H- NATURE CONSERVANCY WAIKAMOI PRESERVE

H- HOSMER'S GROVE

G- NATURE CONSERVANCY KAPUNAKEA PRESERVE

H- HALEAKALA NATIONAL PARK

MAUI

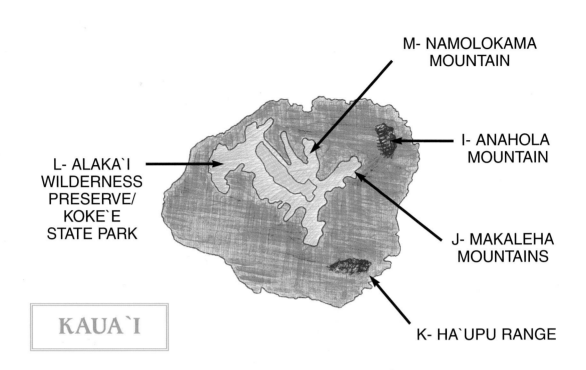

M- NAMOLOKAMA MOUNTAIN

I- ANAHOLA MOUNTAIN

L- ALAKA`I WILDERNESS PRESERVE/ KOKE`E STATE PARK

J- MAKALEHA MOUNTAINS

K- HA`UPU RANGE

KAUA`I

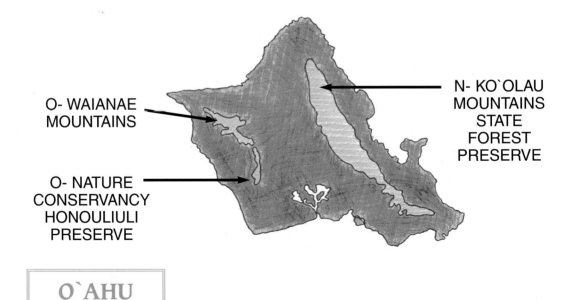

O- WAIANAE MOUNTAINS

N- KO`OLAU MOUNTAINS STATE FOREST PRESERVE

O- NATURE CONSERVANCY HONOULIULI PRESERVE

O`AHU

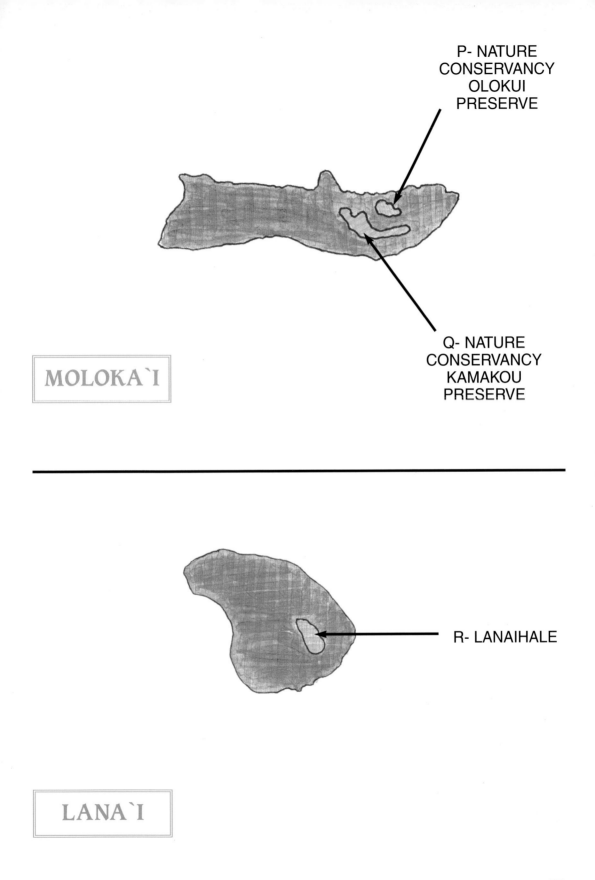

P- NATURE
CONSERVANCY
OLOKUI
PRESERVE

Q- NATURE
CONSERVANCY
KAMAKOU
PRESERVE

MOLOKA`I

R- LANAIHALE

LANA`I

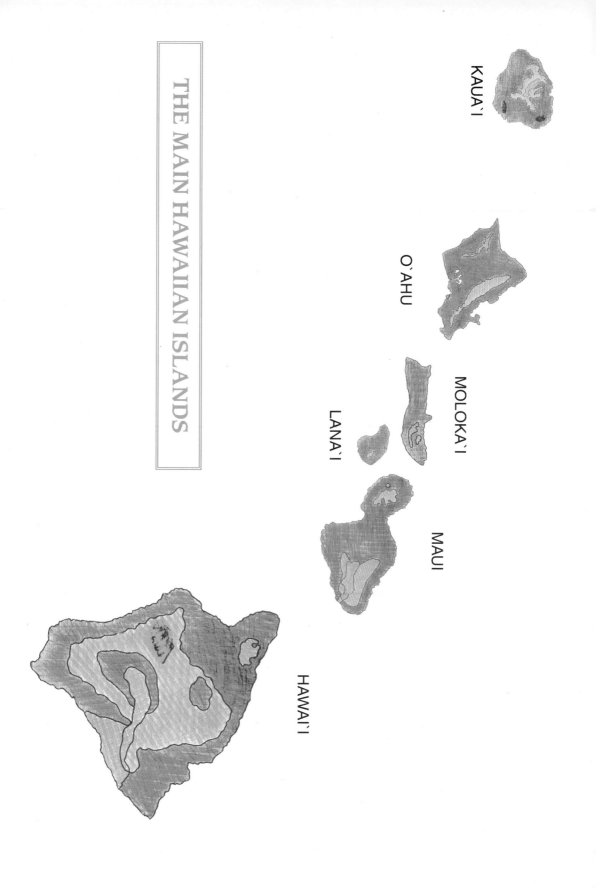

THE MAIN HAWAIIAN ISLANDS

KAUA`I

O`AHU

MOLOKA`I

LANA`I

MAUI

HAWAI`I

Index of Species

References Cited

Hawaii Audubon Society 1993
Hawaiian Birds. 4th edition
Hawaii Audubon Society, Honolulu, Hawai`i. 112 pp.

Wagner, W. L., Herbst, D., and S. H. Sohmer. 1990
Manual of the Flowering Plants of Hawaii
University of Hawaii Press, Bishop Museum Press, Honolulu, Hawai`i. 1,853 pp.

Sohmer, S.H., Gustafson, R. 1987
Plants and Flowers of Hawaii
University of Hawaii Press, Honolulu, Hawai`i. 160 pp.

Neal, M. 1965.
In Gardens of Hawaii
Bishop Museum Press, Honolulu, Hawai`i. 924 pp.

About the Author

Michael Walther earned a Bachelors Degree in Anthropology and Environmental Studies form the University of California, Santa Barbara. He designed and implemented a research project surveying the common native forest birds on Kaua`i and participated in the Po`oli/Nukupu`u study on Maui. His articles and photographs have appeared in Hawai`i Magazine and the Hawai`i Audubon Journal, `Elepaio. First visiting the islands in 1972, The Aloha State is now his home.

Notes

Notes

Notes

Back Cover Photo - A `I`iwi (*Vestiaria coccinea*)
perched in Koli`i (*Trematolobelia kauiensis*).